POETRY

POETRY

*UEA MA
Creative Writing Anthologies
2019*

CONTENTS

VAHNI CAPILDEO	Foreword	VII
TIFFANY ATKINSON	Introduction	IX
HELEN AKERS		2
KIRSTEEN ANDERSON		10
GEFFEN BANKIR		18
RACHEL CLEVERLY		26
LILI COOPER		34
JADE CUTTLE		44
ALISON GRAHAM		52
AMANDA HOLIDAY		58
T. E. IRVINE		66
MARI LAVELLE-HILL		74
DESHAWN MCKINNEY		82
LAIA SALES MERINO		90
RYAN NORMAN		98
Acknowledgements		107

VAHNI CAPILDEO
Foreword

'Knapped' is a satisfying word for the eyes and mouth to handle together. The 'k' used to be audible, in the sharper, more complex beginnings of the pronunciation of this syllable. The consonant cluster simplified over centuries, but still resembles similar words in Dutch and German. 'Knap' echoes the sound of struck flint. The initial letter, silent as a secret, carries a sense of the past. There is a language of stone. Flint nodules that have been quartered, perhaps flaked, perhaps set as flushwork, are a peculiar beauty of many East Anglian buildings. A regular visitor to Norwich could be excused for developing a habit of flintstroking. There are numerous walls where the texture is a mosaic of rough and shiny, hollowed and protuberant. The faces of sunned walls may acquire a natural garnish of moss and flowering stonecrop.

An awareness of flint, the matter of the city, encourages an awareness of the numerous hands which worked it; the ringing sounds of the labour; the sweating, the swearing, the whistling and snacking; precarity, fatigue, hunger; sometimes, accidents; losses; short-term or long-view teamwork, without or with camaraderie. Among the more modern but remarkable buildings of the UEA campus, such as Denys Lasdun's ziggurats, which I have seen channelling rain into a multi-storey run-off – a very 1960s tiered waterfall – there is also a palpable, and now named, sense of the continuing creation of a site, according to differing, but originally learning-centred, visions.

The poetry in this anthology is similarly built. Like its immediate surroundings and connected city, it bears witness to craft. This, if anything, is the UEA 'house style'. Each poet is highly individual in approach, and individuated in voice. What these poets share is an appreciation of language as material. The poems are alive to, and can handle, the weight and implications of other forms. They may imply their own extensibility as litanies, self-revisions, or novels-in-verse. They may insist on the grain of the everyday, setting a recipe askew, or invoking and ripping up the threaded expectations of the bourgeois novel. They do not censor their capacity for metamorphosis, prose poem into body, multilingualism into overt quest for joy. These makers know how carefully altered spacing, recurrent motifs and syncopated rhythms can encourage perceptions of fragmentation and whole to play off each other, sure yet different on every walkthrough.

When I was a student, and writing, not at UEA, and not as part of a creative writing programme, I remember searching for poetic models which would suggest how inner and outer experience are not separate from each other. Deconstruction was the fashion, binaries (which nobody of my background had believed in) were being undone, and 'i' nagged to be lower case. The best and nearest examples I could find were in Old English and Old Norse, which I studied and translated, in lieu of having workshops to attend. I encountered the so-called Seafarer, who knows and experiences bitter and tossing worry amid bitter and tossing elements, not as that most feeble-sounding figure, 'pathetic fallacy', but in an ecology of emotion and environment. He is placed in his troubles and they are placed in him, as dwellings of care, in an affectively untranslatable Anglo-Saxon compound. Trees and cities blossom into their summer aspect, and his wanderlust is set off. They move and suffuse his mood and purpose, not acting as an external inspiration, but partaking, as he does, in a seasonality of quickness. Without a 'writing community' as such, but with a strong sense of the companionship of ghosts, I went on looking, often in the wrong places.

The new and most heartening aspect of the well-crafted poems you will read in this book is, for me, their capacity to express and explore ecologies of feeling and being. Type is made lichen. The poet can be a/part of and in foaming and eroding nature. Here is a gathering of itinerants, who all have been habited in the University of East Anglia's land.

TIFFANY ATKINSON
Introduction

To open with a provocation: in his book *The Hatred of Poetry* (2016), poet and critic Ben Lerner asserts that both readers and writers have always had a love/hate relationship with poetry. His argument runs that while everyone holds a heartfelt notion of what 'poetry' in the abstract could or should be ('love'), when pushed to furnish examples, *actual poems* must always disappoint in the face of the impossible ideal ('hate', or at the very least, discomfort). In summary, he writes:

> Poetry arises from the desire to get beyond the finite and the historical – the human world of violence and difference – and to reach the transcendent or divine. You're moved to write a poem, you feel called upon to sing, because of that transcendent impulse. But as soon as you move from the impulse to the actual poem, the song of the infinite is compromised by the finitude of its terms... Thus the poet is a tragic figure. The poem is always a record of failure.

Is it? Does this doomed enterprise really describe the flexible art that continues to attract a steady and committed readership, and that flourishes in community groups and pub basements and libraries and seminar rooms and performance spaces and social media and, often quietly, sometimes secretly, maybe only once in a blue moon, perhaps once in a lifetime, pretty much everywhere between?

Or could it be that the struggle of the song – for both singer and listener – is also part of its pleasure and richness, coming not from a childish fantasy of having the final word, but from variation and diversity, ingenuity and inventiveness, restlessness and curiosity about what is sayable, what may be seen, thought, touched, heard, conceived in poetic language?

Moreover, as anyone who has attended a poetry workshop will know, the 'move' (or more accurately the series of forays and hunches and trials and reckonings) that must be undertaken for an 'impulse' to become an *actual poem* is not usually felt as a fall from grace, but rather the contrary. All poems start privately, but the process by which they become something independent, a new way of saying, is a productive bewilderment, like conversation, a gain rather than a loss. Every year I learn so much from being part of the challenge and privilege of this process, and every year I am startled afresh by the sheer variety and inventiveness of our students' poems. Let's look at it another way. Actual poems are where we start. Actual poems tell us about what 'poetry' can be. Here is what the class of 2019 has shown us.

This anthology is composed of the latest work from the 2019 cohort of poets studying on UEA's renowned Creative Writing MA.

HELEN AKERS

Helen Akers grew up in Hertfordshire. She has been published in *Smiths Knoll* and *Ink Sweat and Tears*, was awarded first prize in the Wells-next-the-Sea Poetry Competition in 2008, and commended in the Café Writers Pamphlet Commission Competition in 2009. She lives in North Norfolk.

helenja@hotmail.co.uk

Still Pond   (evidence based)

I'm April   I wish so much to fill my head   I'm Andrew   hello hello
we've got a clock that doesn't tick   we're just about to kick off
           Aims: To provide an atmosphere   there's coffee and biscuits!

hopefully you will find one two, maybe all of them   Section 1: What is it?
2: Auto pilot   3: How can it help us relate to our   4: Overview   What next?
             to encourage reflection   *it's been really really useful*

it's a way of distractingyourselfdistractingyourself   it was so
I wasn't able to speak   dog walking   looking at the ground thinking
what's in the freezer?

         lower   your eyelids   be aware   of   your   breath
your   mind   may   become a   no one's   opened
the ginger creams   O my God   this milk doesn't like me   it's curdled

things in my basket   *it's gone*   *it's smashed*   *it's gone*   a sea urchin
it's gone   slate   provokes   memories   of times past   *it's lovely*
Andrew has a conch shell   *you could cut*   pound   scrape with it

Underpinning Attitudes: what on earth am I doing here   looking
at a sea shell?   a Chinese Finger Snap – release   what is stuck to you
accept   release   *whenever I see Tony Blair*   it flares up   flares up

my situation   which I won't go on about   *she is being her own person*   see
we try to force things   tension   pulling a towel   these are my thoughts
no they're not   pull   throw the towel on the bed   relax   Andrew said

a Buddhist monk   can't (there is growing)   offer an opinion   (evidence)
when he hits his thumb with a hammer he might   Andrew said   (it prevents)
talking helps   before   (relapse)   he would rather have cut off his tongue

Piglets

What did Clint Eastwood say? Happy days, over to you,
off with the watering can.   All right for drinks? If you notice
me leaning towards being a Mason just say 'Nah, nah'
bit of a nudge, 'nah'. I'll do what you like, it's faster
than you think. Could you go to the public house
and get me some heroin? If you find me in front of my bike
licking the spokes don't be surprised. If I put my head in a bucket
would you marry me? They said this would happen. Overwhelming
sense of calm, oh fuck off as fast as anything. I might go to bed,
I might not – please don't get a lodger. I've dropped a prune
in a bucket of water. I don't care what I am. Can I just sit here
and mull it over? Holy Sow and the trinity of nipples.
Leave everyone alone. A bit sleepy. I'm just going to write Donna
on my head and rub it off, or not. Don't make me say Goofy again.
Junkies and pickpockets, just trying to snatch a bit of peace.
Mastic Dave and his poor tortured head, and they said one day
you might end up praying to an ashtray. Off we go –
period of silence
                            time shrinks
to something innocuous and there's ten minutes left
to the official tea break. Who makes the tea? Middle-class karate –
excuse me would you mind putting your finger in this hole, I think
I might have drilled through a water pipe. Chop saw – look at that blade,
here we go, hold it tight, keep your thumb out, and that my dear
is how you make a mitre. Fag papers are rather beautiful, like a butterfly.
Lady Guinness is entranced, 'what *is* he doing, what *is he* doing?'
Am I a machinist or a site worker? Hot yoga, bit of breathing, yes
my pulse is racing. One day Goddess, don't be surprised if you find me
doing something rather peculiar in the pantry. I'm going to tinker
with the chop saw, if I flinch it's not a good sign.
In the rather challenging village 'man sips tea' – you know the drill,
tea time!   Oxygen, nostrils; that's as far as I got
with the breathing exercises.   Are you feeling lucky?
Piglets anyone?

The Common Sprung Tape Measure

                      – it seems like a dream that you could ever extend
to determine   the dimensions of ordinary things:
a dado rail   the reveal of a window   skirting board

the tape measure: capable like you of remarkable feats   can ascend
a slope   at any angle passing without harm   over the edge
of a razor blade   (the adult has a hard thin shell)

measurement: you said   *accuracy up to a point*;   *different trades,*
different points   *tolerance*   responsibility for each calibration   (mm)
millimetres   excreting millimetres   sweat   O   spilt

       arteries   of   millimetres   mascaraed   and   glittered
blind   millimetres   expanding   millimetres   contracting
to units   of   arse pucker   and   blink

fingers   of sawdust   lying down   without appetite   in the offcuts
of queasinesss   at the threat of the word   *bespoke*
          – you   have retracted your foot   sealed the aperture

When alarmed they freeze

you are wearing grey boots in bed   so still and setting
setting so still   as concrete setting   liquid concrete
poured   no, no   as still as a squirrel   there are many

(difficult things)   many ways people can mix
(too much energy)   mixed tumbled solidified   as still as
a concrete squirrel   you are as still as   boots

still and grey in bed   like squirrels   but open
to misinterpretation   holding   the perfect idea
behind the mix   for consistency   the perfect mix

for garden ornaments and it's better like this   as squirrels
arboreal scramblers   squirrels leaping slender bodied
on pencil thin branches   but   heavy cloud

as concrete   struggles to move freely   into small details
and small details struggle to flow into long slender bodies
I have found   I have found   3:1 works well

it's recommended for casting   they recommend keeping
them/you   away from the elements   keeping them/you
sheltered   you could even sit in the dark for an hour

they said seasonal variation is a function of fading
but still   they said wait for a gap in the conversation
don't interrupt   holding   holding   the idea behind

they said   burn off energy   in a safe environment
they recommended the perfect concrete idea   they said
not to use your hands when you talk   if necessary sit on them

And sometimes

the reason you can't sleep is obvious –
you can't fit between the doors.
If only I could reverse it. I think it's sleeping
with your vast posterior that's ruining
my Saturday mornings quite frankly.
Pilgrims in August – a distillation of stress.
I was at Jewsons, I can remember the smells.
I went and bought a power drill – shaking.
There's nothing that can be done now.
I thought you'd gone to Yarmouth, Paris –
somewhere with grapes that's easy to get to
on a motorcycle. Am I in purgatory?
O tinnitus! There are two types,
some on the right, some on the left, below.
Some of it keeps you awake. It's just
a case of paying your dues. I don't know
where I cobbled together this sense of ennui –
there'll be another one coming along in a minute.
The harder you work the more exquisite the fag is.
It's getting darker – a bit scared.
This is our honeymoon darling –
if you get a sense of ennui it's something to do.
It's an infinite monkey cage.
It's all becoming clear to me.
Is the cat going to get any bigger or what?
You're just going to feel a bit blue for the day –
there's millions of it all around the world.
What colour catalogue do you want?
Are you having an off day?
You can become ecstatic if you wade around.
Wine gums. So many red ones
but they're not uncomfortable. That's it then –
I just get one moment of rapture?

Unsent Letter

Alone in the storm in New York, you jammed
the zip in the tent, had to cut yourself out.
Dearest, most dear   Mum,   this is hard, looking at my –

If I could tell you: later, knowing you were dying
I kissed you, you said *thank you*. I made you a shirt,
Forget-Me-Not blue sprigged with white flowers.

I walked and sang so long I grew thin, saw the samphire turn
crimson. I looked for the faces of mothers and daughters, and for
all the summers of poppies and cowslips you are with me still.

I stare at the stitches that piece together the squares
of your knitted blanket. My little museum: a flattened cowslip
held in a book, the toy bear with the moth in the freezer.

How considerate you were, your last word *please* – I dream
of your fingers and strands of wool and a thread in the back
of my throat I can't pull out.

KIRSTEEN ANDERSON

Kirsteen Anderson's work as a writer, artist and university teacher places imagination at the heart of both creation and critique. She has published in the fields of French literature and thought, translation and writing the self/personal creativity as integral to student learning. Her artistic practice embraces a range of media.

k.h.r.anderson@qmul.ac.uk

Magnolia

    a magnificence
    that creams
    as winter melts
    into dragging
    spring and fountains
    of carved
    ivory cup
    light
    by the throat

            suspended
            there on day's
            watch a lucifer
            beguiling from japanned
            branches warns
            not to touch
            what is in charge
            of itself

    waxen petal-
    blessing
    that tightens
    to the core
    in gleaming death
    chill skin wrapped
    close on skin
    no space for
    breath

Spring Rhetoric

the world is full
again: trees
contract the air
around a couple
cusped in tight oblivion
as parkland slips
off to its edges

immune to leafy
grandstanding these
lovers concentrate,
heads whitened in a thrift
of blossom

Pro/contra Keats:
engaging with the Anthropoid Sarcophagi in Beirut Museum

Downstairs from a floor noisy with the business
of public display I stumble on silence and slow
time, see you as you are. Freshly asleep
with sheets tucked tight you lie, each
in your well-made bed, so bland I have to ask
what you are for: should art still tranquillise
now that truths are as tough to frame
as beauty?

you've been around long enough to know
what happened here: of war and pock-marked
walls your skin stretched taut in marble
ought to bear at least a trace

                yet nothing of that –
and nothing I can do – disturbs your frigid
style: running my hands the chaste length
of your endless ease leaves you impotent
in the thermostatic shade of your resting-
place, body upon unruffled body retreating
on serried sarcophagi into the bomb-proof
dark of this basement womb

leaves me comforted: fast in your consumer-
cushioned tomb you shirk the fierce work
of centuries, conform art's fortress
against all guns

leaves me bereft: serene, spectacular and dumb,
you speak only through me.

Litter Free

There was a body, stiff
on the street, wrapped
in a pink sheet, rolled
close against the wall
and face to the ground
in a spun-floss cocoon;

and people stood as still
as the shrouded form
– or edged away –
took from the scene
a glimpse of something
like a silkworm, starved;

it was a clean death,
no spreading here
of pale wings, no rising
from a hard grave, not even
a mulberry stain to mark
the pavement.

Dolls

She holds dolls in her head
where folded close they sing
to her not easy
songs
nor lullabies
their fancy
sharpens
her
she has witnesses more knowing
than most waiting
in her night
unruffled *les bonnes*
open-eared
and she unbending
in their shared
clasp

little killers she loves
their trim silence
snugging her stomach
like milk
how blind
under painted lids
and tight in careful gauze
they cannot
breathe
they test

***

                      troublesome

Coppelia

            just loll

                      free and easy

    she hears   squeezy

                            please flex

                these mind-made legs

                    sadlocked hands

                            no she sighs
                            iconic self-
                            contained
                            don't stir or jar me or
                            if you do
                            extract the pieces
                            thoughtfully
                            place me side by side
                            with me
                            put me please back
                            together in the right
                            order no other
                            works as copula
                            hide me
                            bien rangée
                            inside me

                ***

she tucks them up in bed
firm again
from the lesson
of their cold
hard
side
nod

feels herself linked
to the absent
of all dolls

asks: who lay beside you when you were dead?
tasks the blackness

In the Interim

Over each one's skin
each year
as the spring comes
there should be a shimmer
of – scarcely seen
yet jolting as new light –
self-sap,
a coating to wrap and renew
each body
as trees are touched
to life with barely a hint
of green

and since there is not that
there should be
a streaming weft
of turf, sutured
from tensile sod,
that holds harm
out – even from within

and since there is no way
to pause the coiled
certainty of leaves
unfurling, the only trick
is to blunt the end
in a rhythm of fields and hills,
blanketing the body
in a bulwark of land
that consumes it,
smirred with the bitterness
of a limited balm.

GEFFEN BANKIR

Geffen Bankir is a musician, singer-songwriter, artist, and writer. She has a BMus from the Jerusalem Academy of Music and Dance and a LLB from the Hebrew University of Jerusalem Law School, Israel. Geffen is the recipient of the Bryan Heiser Memorial Bursary 2018-19 at UEA.

g.b.redsoil1@gmail.com

Red Soil

I am made of petals.
My eyes are roses petals
my mouth is of daisies

my heart is made of green leaves.
Torn from the tree
before the fall has arrived

when it is fall, they dry up and turn brown.
Then drop to the ground, cover it
in noise that only rats can hear

it is spring, but for me it is fall.
I walk in the same furrows
back and forth back and forth
they are not spiral like the grooves on a 12-inch vinyl
but flat as the pre-heliocentric earth

if only Copernicus, if only, where I walk.
Clods, moist and fresh, cover seeds
that start to sprout

in the fall the soil is barren.
I am laid in red soil
earth is tangled in my hair

I am waiting for the rain.
To come, then the sun,
to wash me over

Celestial Beings (A Love Song)

inhaling aurorae borealis exhaling aurorae australis
inhaling aurorae australis exhaling aurorae borealis
inhaling aurorae borealis exhaling aurorae australis
inhaling aurorae australis exhaling aurorae borealis
inhaling aurorae borealis exhaling aurorae australis
inhaling aurorae australis exhaling aurorae borealis

I'm a servant at your order
I am the master of the work
I submit myself to knowledge
with jim and jones and who knows who
I have a small notebook and some pencils
and I commit myself to the ruler
I find measure to be a good measure
to have when you are at the work
my thumbs are pressed to each other as though they are saying

I am pressed to thee my love we are so alike
my stripes nearly match yours but they turn to the right

they make so much noise (this is what it's like when you are in love)
I keep up the work I serve humbly the throne
inhaling aurorae borealis exhaling aurorae australis
I keep up the work I hold your throne
inhaling aurorae australis exhaling aurorae borealis
I keep up the work I try to be nice so you'll like me
I keep up the work my thumbs get so noisy
I keep up the work I keep up the work I
keep you in sight I keep thinking of you
my thumbs oh my thumbs oh
my oh my so noisy sometimes

inhaling aurorae borealis exhaling aurorae australis
inhaling aurorae australis exhaling aurorae borealis

let it be done please let it be
my thumbs keep bothering me let it be
thumb. let it be thumb. thumb.
we are just so alike

Sometimes

    The velvet skies
They dawn
    on the foggy
        grasses of midday
            where ducks
    nest on cotton balls

Sunshine

    would you give me
        some coins?
Are you over enthusiastic?
    because I'm not
      To look at your
        face , glowing

I love
   you and yours
     will be
I love
   and everything else
        is touched

A row of ducks walking in a line
  A piece of cotton wool attached
        To the third duck's behind.

Rusty Nail

5 petals flower
Three of them in the drawer
Drops of rain fall like Whisky
To an asphalt floor
After we have a quarrel

I hate to think of that but
My room is so lonely
Only me and the ladybugs
Are here, and an occasional
Bumble bee

Why don't you open the drawer?
Why is that so hard?
The lawns shine in the
Afternoon sun and me and I
Who are well acquainted with
this stuff can honestly say

I will drink my Whisky now
Double, with 2 ice cubes
Why are you looking at me
Like that?
Is it because I have a Lady bug
Between my eyes?

Bumble bee and my third eye
Bumble bee is my third eye
Bumble bees and lady bugs
One lost lonely room
I have kicked the drawer open
And all the petals flew away

The ladybugs
They followed
In a formation of 3

read into

       Sometimes when I'm hungry I feel my body is eating
       all its muscles up. It starts with my
       thigh, chewing it slowly, my forehead,
       my knees, then my arms and
       look, I'm missing a toe. But when I'm
       tired

              I want you to be near
       me. I give you a pencil but take the
       paper away. I open the door to my reading
       room but turn off the lights when you
       enter. I hum your favourite song, to
       put you to sleep, but stab your leg
       with my hairpin. I burst into tears when
       you're gone and send you the wet tissue
       closed in an envelope. On the back
       of it I write: I wish I could.

Our Souls Apart

A jug of water. A table. Something white.
Hares, like fur, spread
move in different directions
    The wind
pets them. Then divides.

The fold of the tablecloth
is darker. Like a stain. The water.
I caress the empty jug.

Beautiful, Beautiful
Little hare
Beautiful, Beautiful

Running through the fields in panic
    Is the wind your shelter?

Take me and leave me
Or was it I, leaving
Turning my back on you
So that the wind would not
    Take me away.

RACHEL CLEVERLY

Rachel Cleverly is a part-time poet and full-time worrier. She has featured at Jawdance and Hammersmith Apollo, worked as a New Creative and poet-in-residence at Rich Mix, and read on BBC Radio Norfolk. Her poetry has been shortlisted by *Spread the Word* and *Bad Betty Press*.

Rachelsnc@btinternet.com

It is November 1st in New Cross and

he is awake. I, half-hungover, hear him say
What do people do on a Sunday?
while scratching fake blood
threads stuck to the knit of his chin

        And I remembered when my dog died
        my parents called I left the house
        walked wet circles through town
        on my last loop realised
        boys looked better
        when they were the heat by my feet
        and I wanted to keep wandering
        but I didn't have a job
        and the library was shut
        and I had already finished
        four rounds of the park on my own.

I Dribbled Victory into the Pillow

Our first dinner I didn't eat all day
he told me he was so nervous
had drunk too much wine
to stop melting nerves
he'd forced his food down
I promised myself I would finish
my plate chewed my last bite
slurped down the sauce
his knife and fork entwined
wished I saw his meal
more half empty than half full

>*Are you sticking to your meal plan?*

He'd wanted me to tell him everything
I'd done
vomited
birthdays
film plots
my writing
over the floor of Tesco Express
twenty-seven hours of therapy
got stuck in my throat

>*Part of me wishes*
>*you had a BMI of **.*
>*I could*
>*legally force you*
>*into hospitalisation.*

He asked me to look up bars
thinking I had nothing to do
while he sipped shots
of espresso in the library
found it odd
I got a job waitressing
but never seemed to work

> *Often the ward offers patients this programme*
> *as a means to acquire early leave,*
> *but once they have left we lose all control.*
> *They miss their initial assessment,*
> *are never seen again.*

I asked if we were getting dinner
should I eat before
he was damp like lettuce unsure
replied *work it out on the way*
I threw my phone across the hospital floor

> *St Ann's is one of the only hospitals still using the tube.*
> *We can do this without permission*
> *if the patient is successfully sectioned.*

Our third date I poured white wine
into the grass
of an outdoor cinema
when he asked
if I empty glass
wanted more
I whispered *yes* to the dark

> *A normal diet consists of*
> *a normal breakfast,*
> *a normal lunch,*
> *a normal dinner,*
> *and snacks.*

He drank a pint of milk
each morning after a run
exercise is forbidden
dairy makes me cry

> *Have you seen*
> *the new Louis Theroux?*

He texted *tonight it's you, me and halloumi :)*
I cried through my morning sessions

   I am here.
   I am expressing concern for you.

He was holding up bottles of mixer
Full-fat or Light
I leaked *I don't mind*
he turned his hands over
shifted them up and down
sloshing the fizz
front to back
front to back
Why does it say Light
when they weigh the same
he laughed
my mind bubbled

   I want to apologise on behalf of me and Dr Bland,
   we didn't realise how bad things had got for you.
   I have been around a lot of anxious people,
   they're not nice to be around.
   You are. You hide it so well.

I couldn't pronounce his last name

   Unfortunately I can't prescribe you any form of medication:
   you make good eye contact, don't seem to be nervous
   – I doubt you have any form of anxiety at all.

He stood in my kitchen
pretended to get gin from
down the stairs
but fluid was never his thing
it appeared his shoulders had been
un   hinged

> *Upon finishing the programme*
> *you will not qualify for NHS-funded psychotherapy*
> *for a minimum of six months,*
> *at which point you must rejoin the waiting list,*
> *which may take up to a year.*

His tongue tasted bloody from what he tried
told me he found photos where you could see
sky through my thighs and cried

> *The state of the NHS is ridiculous.*

Then sipped the brown from my tea

> *You're only twenty-two.*

Last week he asked
Is there anything you haven't told me?

> *And still no periods?*
> *And still no periods?*
> *And still no periods?*
> *And still no periods?*
> *And still no periods?*

Terminal A

In the airport queue, Dad hands me a *cantuccini*: I bite.
It is twelve o'clock. I have taken time off to get fat
with my family. I have not being making the right choices.

Tomorrow I will trace a path   follow a therapist to the   get lost in all the
hot food/   salad bar/   hot food/   salad bar/   hot food/   salad
bar/
    Sandwich   sandwich   sandwich

Three people back in the queue, I watch a *signorina*
survey the cafe's *biologico* aisle, pulling at the shell
of her almond lips. Eyes fly over packets:

SenzaGlutineSenzaUovaSenzaLatteSenzaGlutineSenzaUovaSenzaLatte
SenzaGlutineSenzaUovaSenzaLatteSenzaGlutineSenzaUovaSenzaLatte
SenzaGlutineSenzaUovaSenzaLatteSenzaGlutineSenzaUovaSenzaLatte
SenzaGlutineSenzaUovaSenzaLatteSenzaGlutineSenzaUovaSenzaLatte
SenzaGlutineSenzaUovaSenzaLatteSenzaGlutineSenzaUovaSenzaLatte

Biscuits scream *vegano* *vegano* *vegano*
above the crying planes outside. She

picks up/   flips seals/   picks up/   flips seals/   picks up/   flips seals/
  checks calories   checks calories   checks calories

Flight Boarding. It is ten past twelve.
In the hospital someone makes a choice.

She puts the biscuits back on the bottom shelf.

Panettone

The sponge was smack in the middle of the red table mat.
His mum slow motion slices it in two.

Just tell me when – Not too much! I cut in, too loud.
I am watched by seven pairs of eyes, barely blunter than the blade.

A sister leans back; two brothers lean in.
His mum thrusts metal down into the thick fluff of the cake.

The knife pierces raisins, ripping clean lines between dish and sponge.
Burnt sugar edges are cut jagged, deformed.

His dad pushes blue china below her shaking hand.
The slice looks much bigger, plated and placed in front of me.

My uncle sent a panettone each Christmas by post.
Once, the delivery man dropped the sponge.

My mum chased it, cursing the circle shape of the tin.
I heard her shriek as it slipped down the hall.

It rolled into the living room, cut the corner of the sofa;
it rolled into the dining room, and slipped beneath the table cloth.

The sponge was stopped by the outstretched leg of a dining chair.
We built nets of napkins for catching crumbs, opened the tin, ate with
    our hands.

I look down at the table, his mum's still slab of cake. No one watching.
I thrust a fork in: slide a slice off my plate to the floor.

LILI COOPER

Lili Cooper has been writing at UEA for four years and hopes to pursue a career in London. Her poems utilise hybrid forms to explore how words want to be stretched and heard. She has read her poems for BBC Radio Norfolk and her instagram alter ego can be found @myflfalsefldiary.

lili.cooper12@icloud.com

Deadliest Catch

        Dragged a net of fish   The sheet hiding high
      Down trousers like the   Puddles a red beckoning
Edge of a bed wrapped around   Seat leather's curse sting
         Ankles into hospitals   On the legs down stitches
           Ears when eating   A lunch of lochs rises
Fold away extremities in case   Organs laundering questions
       Of any other screams   This illness is a
          Quiet fills bowls   Brine of bruises
          With hot bellies   Folded into squares of
     Sauce on sweater's chin   Tilled & naked silence
      Goes choo choo stain   Teeth under the chatter of wisdom
Slipped in the pile of washing   Crawling to puncture
Mackerel eyes flame in wicker   This teardrop of fish skin
    There is wet at the seams   The stiff eyelashes catch
                  Alight & crumble
              Against the backdrop
              of accidental spillage
                 these are not
                 knickers! but
             Adult terms that slip
               Under hands &
                    thread
                Lips in them
              Lace is nets to
              Snag lovers this
            Soreness is a snag
           This is more than a
            Sore this is a tear
          The thorn heals but
            won't stop crying
             Fire on its way
            Down don't well
             Will not show
                 here are
                  flames
                  instead
                    Yell-
                      ing

God-bye

god is dying down
at the bottom of the garden
where the chicken wire
isn't hexagons anymore but open to foxes –
mum buries her this time,
though it's usually dad
digging & crying

now the ground is frozen under
the Christmas stump
& the hole can only be a foot or so deep –
they gather into prayer, plant her there – say,
she was a good'un
a reminder of the then flowers
the June that crushed her
into a smell & sound of bulbs
popping rose water
tendered out jars
coins in clinking abandon,
flying butter pushed into fairy heads

still – I find her cut-out wings
around the place
like doilies laying themselves under
sponges, quiet & decorative
as her washing-up gloves' fur trim

she died in the corner over there but folds away so
neatly in the Bible, her flattened calling
clover & pressed crumbs
under the lofty table –
words I am unfit
to eat but still
I can taste
her lawnmower's icing sugar

& in all the commotion
of hard winter I feed her final
morsels of stale hope to the robins
so their bellies go on
being red
make a
bonfire of pages so our cheeks ripen with laughter
                              & it all blows over us

Background

Stories depend on what happens next. They go on. They don't get stuck to plates or lost under fridges. They ride out on horses. They never walk or take the bus. They get in quickly and out quicker. They don't chat. They never give hugs. They are not frivolous. They make decisions behind giant doors in suits. They close cases. They never smile or wave. They do not underline. They do not eat sandwiches in public. They are stronger than stone. They don't have time to write diaries, addresses or lists. They don't own highlighters or Post-its. They have no comments in the margins. They make speeches without cue cards and exit brisk stage left. They follow a plot. They do not drink or wash their clothes. They have never used a toilet brush. They do not cry. They press on. They are not born, they begin, middle and end. They never talk about themselves but make brisk dialogue that gets straight to the point.

Stories depend on what happens next: in short, they go on. When all their answers are satisfied, they smile at their audience, close their books and put their feet up on the ottoman. They sink into their comfortable chair with pride. The faceless background wobbles in with her tray of tea and biscuits, she hangs there, teacups shaking. They help themselves.

Get your shame face on

i lug around my body
but get tired a lot of its sh*t & sit
down on benches *donated by anonymous* the bin is full to brim with
    cigarette
butts & i recognise my little name in the way trashcan
sounds to a Brit clunky &
de-fluff the dryer –   my favourite chore
                there is something living inside there
                i try to pin it to the pane
of my sunglasses & stare through it
but obscurity   shatters my legs to wobble & –
maybe i'll wee   dogs do &
                people like them just fine – i am just as exposed
as cocking in the Mr Blobby suit
i got second hand   car boots are lovely
reminders of everyone dying
to leave a legacy of things plastic
i often think 'greed' is a funny concept –
    my liver grumbles more than my stomach now
i dance myself into shards   prismatise the blobs of my
            soft nakedness into headspin
& vomit towards really
wanting to demand of my mum if
she thinks i'm crazy

but it's late & she works hard so – i'll shut up then
i lay awake feeling the stars   might crash
into my brain   this is how babies must feel
about mobiles –
tableaus relax themselves
into my eyelids with   alarmingly subtle
hellishness & my sister comforts me to dawn
gleaning through tobacco
            like a swan over greasy water
i want to burst with fear
like a spider's egg & build myself back together in a satisfyingly

complete restoration project
the f**king dread of that tune
naming every dog for every letter of the alphabet
but naming makes me worry who i am
except *you've been here before* pipes up
it's so reassuringly odd to slip
                                 down life again
                                        like a f**king banana skin in Mario Kart
in this sly mistake of sunshine
surely too sweaty to be pleasant

A Recipe for Good Poetry is Impossible to Follow

1. Start with onions. In the beginning, they are everything. Classically, they will try to make you cry, because they are bullies. A tip to not show weakness: breathe through your nose and cement your tongue to the roof of your mouth. NEVER confess any secrets. Just remember they are the key element to flavour so submit to them. Open a window if you have to or escape to the loo. Large chunks should do. When they are laid in the olive oil laugh at their sizzling deposition. Shout all the swear words you can remember.
2. Celery will be muddy if it is grown outside, this is good. Unmuddied celery is grown in bathtubs in the Netherlands like pharmaceuticals are cooked. Here, it is better for things to remain organic. You see, naturally inspired ingredients are pulled by the fingers of divine hands, which make work lighter and taste stronger. Hold the stalks in your grip like fingers. Shave their legs so they are presentable and cube them. Keep the leaves for later. This is important. Nothing should be wasted in the process.
3. Garlic resin is sticky like amber or semen. It thins the blood which often feels alarmingly poisonous. Leave this resin on your hands to remind you of what has been shed. The smell may haunt you for a few days. But it passes, like everything, eventually. Your veins should race with the extra iron, you will develop a superpower you are unaware of. Read all the recipes before you make the decision.
4. A good celeriac should resemble a baby's head when it first appears. You should not want to put her down. This is how you know you have chosen quality produce. The soiled tendrils will be her hair, her shape the cuteness of plump, the gnarled peel her unconditional visage of love. Hold her in your arms and rock until she gurgles to sleep, this should take around 15 mins. When she is down, anoint her head with water, then peel and chop into chunks. Inside, you will find she has a texture like soft. Try not to cry. It will add extra salt. She is not real except for when you need her, like the sets of houses in sitcoms. A man will escort you to let off a balloon. If it is red it will be better. Share with yourself the sign of the peace. Perform the sacrament of yourself silently. Always remember, real character is crucial to a delicious end result, so sacrifice is paramount.

5. Now take the celery leaves you saved from earlier. They are the newspaper for this fire. Flame up the snapped wicker until it smells like fennel. This is called therapeutic. Empty your bladder. Caress yourself under the tap like a burn.
6. Add butter, the ancient remedy for grief, for it contains the unsung milk of baby animals which everyone knows are the epitome of innocence. Rub it over your fingers to remove the garlic blood. Say a blessing and the smell should go quicker. Add water. Pick wild flowers for the windows.
7. Finally, stock cube. Watch it dissipate in the silvery landscape. Watch the salt whirl out like jam into porridge. Watch the arrow hit the spot of deliciousness like a pill cures. Leave to simmer, until everything is denatured and original again.
8. Blend. The sound is what you won't forget. Belt out Jerusalem if you can as you fuse away all wholeness with your purifier. Once it is smooth you will be born again. The fewer lumps, the more easily it will go down. Unification is necessary. But transubstantiation is sometimes difficult to swallow. If so, add a little more garlic and you will believe in the power of the trinity.
9. Grate nutmeg to taste. Force yourself to look once at the sickening texture of her brain. Hold her head to your nose and breathe until you want to start letting go. Put her under your pillow, then spit out her taste like vomit and take the bin straight out. The less you are reminded of the brain the better and she adds an excellent profile flavour.
10. Eat up. Until you are so full you can't feel. Bathe your body in the soup to make a pure celeriac of your heart. Put the leftovers into a can and save for moments of delicious guilt.

This condensed jelly is of course good poetry

*a choppable cylinder of abstraction, corned beef, pepper & beads of table
sweat mixed with mash touching people's hearts dressed as cards
copying each other's cheat as they shuffle to magic's eternal
ditty with their tongues out spelling antidote's shape as if
cure is a pure perfection of grammar as if
remedy is every answer instead there
is no making way out no creating
a mirror to slip away only a step for a moment
of cigarette stillness instead of multiplying beyond
this middle become the slender apply pressure to the
navel hoping leaking will go back up proliferation will go
back inside for heat is entropy that reduces but will eventually
turn its face over to coldness & keep pouring letters until dilution
until this mess is all is red where drain was there is no umbrella in this flood
no Noah no Dove*

JADE CUTTLE

Jade Cuttle, Cambridge graduate and Deputy Poetry Editor at *Ambit*, has written for BBC Radio 3, BBC Proms, BBC Introducing, *TLS* and *The Guardian*. Jade is also a singer-songwriter, releasing an album of poem-songs through Warren Records in 2019 with funding and support from PRS Foundation and Make Noise.

jadecuttle@hotmail.co.uk

A manifesto: towards a poetics of escape
The page is a prison

i.

let me escape the law of language
let me turn the key until it breaks
                until it rusts
                until the poetic truth locked within the skin of words
seeps out
                    words as cage
                        the agonising chafe
                              the storm against the glass – let it in

ii.

let me cast the lyric 'I' away from the crowd of words that keep it warm
                      blindly bowing down beneath its totemic authority
let me denounce the false sense of fixity locked within the lyric 'I'
let me interrogate the lyric 'I' left stranded and shivering without a stage[1]

iii.

let me reject the white narrative of the page
        eject myself out from its claws
let me ignore the sore red frenzy of spellchecker
        as I rewrite the
                white

---

[1] Each time a poet chooses to package their identity into the narrow confines of the lyric 'I', they prioritise to inhabit one of their potential identities over another. But the endless contradictions of identity can never be flat-packed into one single neat space. The self is constantly created anew with each new encounter, each new experience, and each new thought. We are not the same people we were yesterday, and perform different versions of ourselves depending on our entourage.

I slip out from my
lift the latch and leave
the door unlocked I don't care
what blows in behind me
these ribs of bow and arrow
would fire away its fruit but
the flies have got there first

skin skin skin skin skin skin skin skin skin skin
skin skin skin skin skin skin skin skin skin skin
skin skin skin skin skin skin skin skin skin skin
skin skin skin skin skin skin skin skin skin skin
skin skin skin skin skin skin skin skin skin skin
skin skin skin skin skin skin skin skin skin skin
skin skin skin skin skin skin skin skin skin skin

skin skin skin skin skin skin skin skin skin skin skin skin skin skin
skin skin skin skin skin skin skin skin skin skin skin skin skin skin
skin skin skin skin skin skin skin skin skin skin skin skin skin skin
skin skin skin skin skin skin skin skin skin skin skin skin skin skin
skin skin skin skin skin skin skin skin skin skin skin skin skin skin
skin skin skin skin skin skin skin skin skin skin skin skin skin skin
skin skin skin skin skin skin skin skin skin skin skin skin skin skin
skin skin skin skin skin skin skin skin skin skin skin skin skin skin
skin skin skin skin skin skin skin skin skin skin skin skin skin skin
skin skin skin skin skin skin skin skin skin skin skin skin skin skin
skin skin skin skin skin skin skin skin skin skin skin skin skin skin
skin skin skin skin skin skin skin skin skin skin skin skin skin skin
skin skin skin skin skin skin skin skin skin skin skin skin skin skin
skin skin skin skin skin skin skin skin skin skin skin skin skin skin
skin skin skin skin skin skin skin skin skin skin skin skin skin skin
skin skin skin skin skin skin skin skin skin skin skin skin skin skin
skin skin skin skin skin skin skin skin skin skin skin skin skin skin
skin skin skin skin skin skin skin skin skin skin skin skin skin skin
skin skin skin skin skin skin skin skin skin skin skin skin skin skin

skin skin skin skin skin skin skin skin skin
skin skin skin skin skin skin skin skin skin
skin skin skin skin skin skin skin skin skin
skin skin skin skin skin skin skin skin skin
skin skin skin skin skin skin skin skin skin
skin skin skin skin skin skin skin skin skin

I had been coughing up mud
into the sinks of strangers
until they put salt down
on my tongue how kind
I thought when the slip-ups
stopped and teeth lined up
silent as a dry stone wall.

Moulin Rouge

I sent my heart to the slaughterhouse, but it ended up at the meatworks, the place where scraps unfit for human consumption go. The knacker's yard. Knowing men in bloody overalls will peg me up to their podium with all the other gristle trophies, stripped back to the pink blush of meat kept in line by the knife's edge. A moulin rouge of frenzy, spinning poses of panic in neat and naked rows, a salle de spectacle that enthrals but not enough, destined for the freezer, awaiting permission to thaw. But then I changed my mind about the whole putain de cabaret and requested my heart be sent back first class, which it was, a little shaken and peg-grazed but still intact, barely a bruise despite its pirouettes. I'll pick away the sores but I worry that once I start I won't be able to stop like how maggots given half a chance will chew their way through marrow until all that's left is a string of holes only the wind blows through.

Décolleté

If skin is supposed to hang neatly off the shoulders, snug as a summer blouse with room to breathe and barter, delicate as a décolleté (not to be confused with decollate which means 'to behead') then I think mine needs sending back. It has started to snag around the elbows and split; spindles poking through to tamper with the day, wire framework rusting in the sunlight. Sometimes these bones gallop at such a speed it's difficult to keep up. I've forgotten my skin on a train seat more than once, sized up by a stranger who smiles then hands it back, mademoiselle? I've left it slung across the back seat of a taxi, dumped at a soirée, in cloakrooms and countless métros, but it's always sent straight back to my front door. This décalage between my bones and its business leaves me hors de soi: not quite here, not quite there, voyaging on an out-of-date passeporte, eyes like two moons shunted out of orbit, rolling back into their sockets to search for clues.

Towards a Poetics of Escape

A heart of lichen will latch onto anything
let its roots fall slack

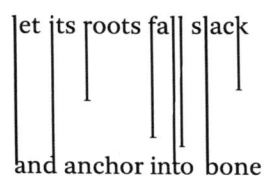

and anchor into bone

Algal Bloom

head submerged
eyes glazed with salt
I'm caught between the bloom
and scum in this rock pool's
wide untaken palm
wet knuckles
capped with cockles
clap wildly as each new wave
washes me in and out from a body
that just wants to break
upon the shore
dragged by the high tide
of hope that lichen might latch on
and anchor down into bone
I let my grip falter
and loose film
of skin
becomes foam
so dip your toes in
but don't go the distance
like each bloom that came before
I am phosphate dead zone
where hearts flicker
and fail
septic waste
whose taste is bad
you can boil me down
but the toxins will remain
neither fire nor flood
will kill me
either [2]

---

[2] Algal blooms can last from a few days to many months.

ALISON GRAHAM

Alison Graham is a poet and essayist whose poetry has appeared in *Bare Fiction*, *Datableed*, *Zeno Magazine*, and *3AM Magazine*. She has an essay called 'by luck of the harbour' forthcoming from *Seam Editions*, and can be found on Twitter as @A_Graham.

alison_graham_@hotmail.co.uk.

from *Wreathing*

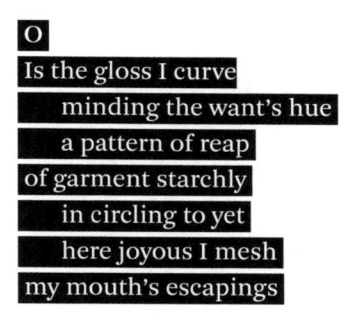

> **O**
> Is the gloss I curve
> minding the want's hue
> a pattern of reap
> of garment starchly
> in circling to yet
> here joyous I mesh
> my mouth's escapings

Out from by crypt at first meeting
{
I roil into a future gone under
day passing over my forehead in trail
drooping gold   a reasonable of gold
           inert of seeming and southerly   goes
witness who do I talk the phone bleats foam-
ing sound   still I tilt but spin   how?   not to ask
or source   in circling settle into from
this old varying place I start   a kind
like exacting coat   lining of which to
unstructure   all about the currency
of the living yet to come   to do with you
           no omit that from here on my yearn was
shook it out mineral foil some body
bed always bed to leave or bring you valley

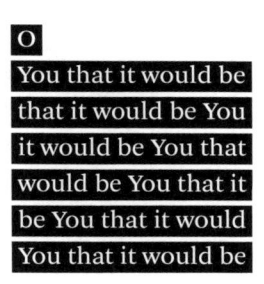

> **O**
> You that it would be
> that it would be You
> it would be You that
> would be You that it
> be You that it would
> You that it would be

> O
> If titled it would
> only be glamour
> upon this a jump
> to avoid or self-
> supporting arch o-
> ver to title would
> be ease an eclipse
> or obliterate
> |
> O
> in a valley more
> imagined where
> fitful the grammars
> while inelegant
>   the draw a labour
> most decent here goes
> handful scattered
> and desiccate in
> which I am spitting

Getting to the many actuals
{
Birdugly tone sanding facet of sky
    has as target a struck and eyeless thee
    and thou in extreme dawning to hourly
jut of marvel   nevertheless comes
gift of to be lost   climate as this
grasses lengthen   and in number enough
for thee as opposed to thou   and I
have known an equator or three in these
times   is formidable   a trilling
conjure   won't it   a grove   plucked stark
    feverish effort to tend and to coil
distances into purple   to budding
    horned as it is   face in a twist   being
without sleep a multiplex of seasons

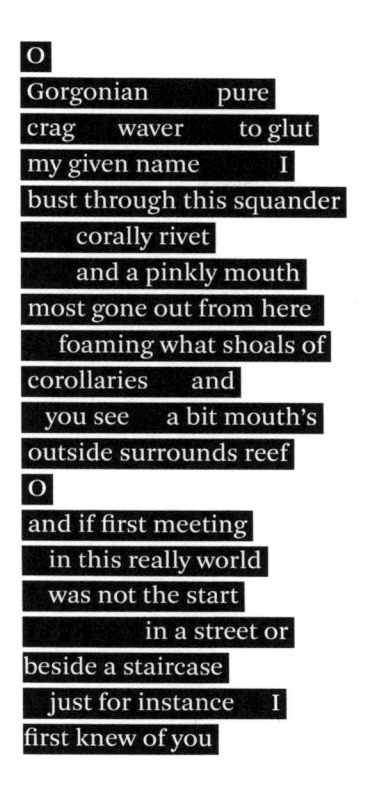

> O
> Gorgonian   pure
> crag   waver   to glut
> my given name   I
> bust through this squander
>   corally rivet
>   and a pinkly mouth
> most gone out from here
>   foaming what shoals of
> corollaries   and
>   you see   a bit mouth's
> outside surrounds reef
> O
> and if first meeting
>   in this really world
>   was not the start
>   in a street or
> beside a staircase
>   just for instance   I
> first knew of you

You as entirely apart from the end of land
{
Light as a roadmark   toll upon the breath
        applied in daubing gesture   the gesture
interrupted   the sun such that I keep
expecting   the light   in a field   fosters
condition for wilded cows   their lowing
splits indelible to newness   now I
propose terraced houses   road medium
width   five eighteen watery dusk   I put
bluely fearings to cease   have put human
feeling to farmed beasts   vow to carry
no drystone on over a part from cliffside
where samphire is taken and it tastes   I
lie not   more of the sea than the actual
or more of steepings come over the land

O
  and jagged the movement
  of people about
me taken with you
  though I was off to
elsewhere I could when
turned away know
an outstretch of ferns
frothing in my coat

AMANDA HOLIDAY

Amanda Holiday completed a degree in Fine Art before moving into film, directing shorts for the Arts Council, BFI and Channel 4. Between 2001–10 she lived in Cape Town where she worked in educational television. Her chapbook *The Art Poems* was published in 2018.

www.amandaholiday.com
amandabholiday@gmail.com

The mother who left her baby for the Queen

the baby cried very little –
he had been home two days
milk in her breast, one feed
the house was hollow

she wrapped him in brown paper
inside a fleece. 5 am at the bus stop
waiting. London was still.

In Pall Mall taxis churred on tarmac
streetlamps blinked

at Buckingham Palace gate
she laid him down and walked away.

He would stride back, one day
with brass bands blasting,
jet planes icing the sky
in red and blue plumes
a million plastic flags
fanning the new king –
her baby, grown so tall

I saw her on the bus today –
same face, pale and yellow

as twenty years ago,
splashed across the papers

sea diss

        wanton waves of blithery mithery
        flowebbing forth and back and fifth
        seepage world-wide meddlesay
        Maersk tankards rusting bye-ships
        lull wet yarners here-a-pebble
        carry noot underwalkers from the
        Cape black stacked weedies halloo hay
        Simons Town, Muizenberg, False Bay
        unt Cape Point atta horizon
        bends right in the middle   a bit

Melasma

On this face a pool stain residue
blot-soaked skin spreading to cheek
and eyebrow. Rorschach teabag compress.
Apple cider vinegar, aged,
freckled swamp mulatta.
Every day new parts of the map –
islands, cul de sacs, U-turns,
superhighways scrubland,
indigenous growth, decolonial mulch,
browning toxic vitiligo.

This is what happens.

Camberwell cabbagey and cold,
giant daddy long legs skim zip wires in the dusk.
Smoke alarms pick out screams across the gardens.

sickhead

        goes without saying
     good to write   poems when ill
   full of phlegm   mucus or pus words,
 everyone reading will recoil and   retch
stick in the throat catarrh   twanging raspy karrkk karrkk
skanky three-legged skunk *sickhead* pops up everywhere on the roof
spitty jizz luminous curds of snot whey elastic strings
 glutinous   albumen snap-back

Out out foul grot. Cough it up. Spit it out
  knees up mother. Thy will be done.
    snags of lung skin discarded tissue germ-addled in corners mouldering   two tablets[1]

Nah man. Grim Bronchial Whoop whoop.
   Brexit bulk buy antibiotics
     Strepsils Wintergreen Fisherman's friends
     gasp Calpol
       poetry transcends flu,
         minor ailments
         and sickness

---

1 worked hard for this poem now go out and git your own poem

Mandalay Bay

1900 bullets packed

                                  no questions asked
2 dozen guns   straight up in the lift
all AK automatics   to the 32nd floor
                                of the Mandalay Bay Hotel
                                checked in
not in his name

                                a white male, 64

& when the concert blasted
down below outside
                                first he smashed out
                                the glass – east and south
                                then took his perch
birds-eye

                                and trained the barrel down

The angel had rushed ahead
to warn them – Blackapina ran
frenzied through the crowd –
Y'all going to die tonight   Mad madzinga

happy people dancing on
faraway the noise, the music.

                                His first round kissed and popped,
                                swatted the distant skirmish
Perhaps he was too far?
                                After 3 rounds, sea change
The music stopped:
screams, the air chilled
She pointed at the mirror wall
He's up there! Some nut!

                        He turned automaton
                        unthinking, Armageddon

                        None of it is true, none of us
                        is true. Nothing matters

                        load and shoot and load again
                        old hands tired with holding

                        We're breaking down

                        and another round
                        pop pop pop pop

Aint this what Potus meant?

                        turn and point deadened

                        And time closed in
                        he knew outside
                        they came creeping
                        in hall and stair and lift

                        and still it didn't matter

                        for that last click
                        he sucked gun metal   Dead end.

on TV – Breaking news:
a massacre

& from the twisted vessel
of Potus's throat his
words distort and twang;

Our bonds cannot be broken by violence
                        America comes together as one

T. E. IRVINE

T. E. Irvine is a Derbyshire-born poet, but now lives in Hertfordshire where he co-runs a spoken word evening Shout or Whisper. His poetry is primarily interested in the emotional and psychological aftereffects of our youth (whilst pushing the thresholds of form). His work can be found in *The New Luciad*, *Ink Sweat and Tears*, *We Are All Somebody* and *Bridge: The Bluffton University Literary Journal*.

thomasirvine1995@gmail.com

Sisyphus, happy

enough to fill a heart, such shallow reliefs left behind with every crafted
downwarding desire path
mapped and given further groove, rock
revelling in its own roughandtumble
nature, inhale, return to summit,
repeat, let the same wrecked sky wash out day's damages, to call my
pushing futile is to call
rain cruel in its duty to fall, i call it
a deep love affair with gravity,
adoration for repetitive strain,
if torture is purpose then this is conventional agony, never pressed to
hold Heavens
or grow another liver overnight, i'm
all right building Romes in my
afternoons, in another life
i was a pensive roof-tiler knowing his day was done when the rain no
longer reached the floorboards, in another life
i combed beach-hair for daily debris
clapping for myself when seawater
ran clean through sand without catching on a single knot, i'm no hero i'm
a ninetofive kinda-guy happily bookmarked
by another moon running slopesided
down a dawn, or heavy morning sun
dragged out by the skin of its beams, my hands earn their next callous
and soak in the rainfall thirsty, attempt to save it
from the harassment of carrying another
mineral, my priceless life, i'll take
time on the downward, let blood rush back to its fractures, pick a
few rough mountain flowers, study
the slight indents i've designed and
left behind, used to treat myself
with glimpse over the verge, a running start but death seemed
sadder than structure, and who then would
raise the boulder, i know stone
in all its familiar grinds and
fallow crooks, whether carried or caressed, my sweet ageing

backwards bouncing baby boulder
holding a little lighter, a little
cleaner with every heave,
often encouraged to walk upwards steadied my push or
sometimes light enough to cosy in my back's
small, bonding over what pull feels
like, that icarusintimacy, and
when it settles on our skin we'll know downpour
as a return, a reach to make and reward of
reaching, the heavy yet measured
step back to summit,
decanting slowly, pick a few more mountain
flowers, reward with a thought, taste the
falling cascade, renew;
the struggle, imagine

Soft Machine (in Summer skin)

humid saccharine on cheek; motherfuss.   a spitful of dandelion parachutes, a
blackbird philharmonic, watertaste from   outside tap. nobody   then everybody
knows   pedal without further gravelling elbow scores.   your driveway an
incline   takes a little longer, everyone else leaves; giggles distantly. instead alone,
spinning wheels upturned, prick a finger between spokes,   throb.   chalk mural
pavement washed away by a Wednesday; whole cul-de-sac cries.   only way to
wring out grass stains from forearm is via snakebite,   girl next door draws blood.

once, someone said smoke lives in between friction and twigs,   all you did was skin
away to a sage underbelly,   felt cruel. have you ever shattered a paper plate? unsure what it is
about wine   makes men cry, mantra-ing all over your shoulder *remember what young*
feels. you don't know it by anything yet, other than dockleaf soothe,   a few
summers later, wine-inspired, a whole August will be ruined by a wrong someone kissing your
eyelid closed for   first time. sports car with no middle seatbelt; lean into
corners, *braced* a natural state;   somehow feels right to die on a Sunday. burnt cd copy
of jumpy and scratch, red and orange songs. a balloon escapes through sunroof as family
unisongasp. nothing to hold on to,   almost everybody laughing.

Soft Machine (in Winter skin)

sweat through cotton, collecting in purlicue lining of old loosefitted mitten; handmedown sores.   a pitying of carol singers, a stocking-sized insistence hanging from fireplace. each inhale   soggy, each exhale   stab, nostrils hurt with their circles reddening, pink as ceramic hob rings, Saturn belts,   tissue roughtug at the sniff. someone once said Christmas lights were parasitic, or maybe mistletoe.   spend family dinners chewing tongue into ulcers   (polite alternative to politics),   watch your parents fall asleep   fire on. later, dream about carrying them to separate beds as they feign sleep, unsubtle smilings.   have you ever woken up thinking the house was on fire?

everything seems smaller than you remember.   once, doctor said you'll grow as tall as dad wow *a giant* everyone laugh,   now he's got few staircases left in him, walks in disquiet spasm, hard not to interrogate every buckle as knee's last embarrassment.   beard grows out now, banish a grey hair   two more take its place, pluck a third   spot balds,   body exercising its first *no* all stubborn todderlike. mull over crosses on calendar,   promise you'll buy a diary this time.   it is as quickly Christmas as it isn't. backgrounding of gunpowder, it is midnight   everyone sorry for something. another year, another mousetrap hurries shut   either on the mouse or its spoils.

Kubrick with a Kodak (Through a Different Lens)

I. (Lovers on a NY Fire Escape, 1946)

      unchaperoned evening
         you don't need to see – jesus
            that jawline could cut right
               through July but what's hotter, cold
                  steel against the bare knee
                     or the way he pronounces
                        his home state on your neck?
                          tell me where you're from again

II. (How People Look to Monkeys, 1946)

my bars are seized	a savage grasp
with thumbs that bend	inwards wrapped around
the small ones pulling	the big ones short-haired
shrieking faces covered	tears spittle ice cream
shoulders hunched canines	baring hooting and howling
matted hair nostrils flared	the smell of sex dirty air
some say we're related	my distant cousins but
they're just the lucky ones	who won history
in the bigger cage	they await the proof –
with bated breath	the cameras flash
I scratch my ass	the crowd goes *wild*

III. (A Serviceman Passes the Time at a Handwriting Analysis Booth, 1947)

    Each letter stands to attention,
    upright and conscribed capitals.
    Perhaps you signed schoolwork like that
    or maybe it was something trained
    beneath sirens, an urgency
    to outlast ink and meet the haunt
    of a picture you've never met,
    safe inside a heart-shield bible –

    a machine told you all of this?
    I just wanted to learn cursive,
    I just wanted to teach my wrist
    leanings of a softer weapon.

IV. (Two Girls Adjusting their Hearing Aids, 1948)

It's funny when it's Charlie
        and the Mighty Wurlitzer,
roller-skates and a lion's cage
        and omnilingual eyebrows

but there are no intertitles here,
        nothing but a monochromic hum.
Sad clowns in the streets, with their drooping
        frowns and rounded vowels like compressed howls;

These fit in your pocket look they come in gold
        you help me with mine and I'll help you with yours
a tiny squeal, strangled birdsong, and then –
        we laugh at our laughter's sound in the mirror.

MARI LAVELLE-HILL

Mari Lavelle-Hill is a poet person. She has previously been published in magazines *HVTN* and *Lucent Dreaming* and online at *Blue Agave*. She has also been published in the anthology *Volta: An Obscurity of Poets* and in UEA's 2017 and 2018 undergraduate anthologies. She occasionally tweets @MariLavelleHill.

mlavellehill@gmail.com.

O Law

      hemmed between
brand-new breton stripes
I find your name   sound it out
all the vowels trembling long &
I hear it   moving through the tracks
where a pheasant waits at a railway crossing
more patient than bridges   I hear it when
the spinning wind turbines think for a minute
gently synchronise & for a second
     I'm hardly here at all

everyone's got this thing
about death & it follows me   softly   audaciously
like a gold volvo in the bike lane
in the newspaper today it says:
girl made cookies with grandmother's
ashes   handed them out in class
I wonder how my granny tastes if it's
anything like your name
which I still suck on   privately

     I keep unravelling vowels
a long spool   which I knit
into a cardigan for myself   *are you cold?*
my family ask   so pink &   happy
video-calling me from their holiday
my mother has a glass of ice
in front of her   bites down occasionally
I am scared she will swallow
her cracked crown whole   back to dirge theme

I saw a hedgehog with his bristles
burnt off & he looked just like me
hiding in a bonfire
     maybe being happy is just
not thinking about   being happy
I have headphones that click
when I watch films where there is a dip
in sound   no mouths move & I never
noticed all the silence before

    now it rides over me
the brief assurance of my twenties
lapping gently at my round
tummy damp trackies at the offie
I buy four cans   each with your name on
I drink them all down *yes* *the sentencing*
papers came through & back from holiday
my mum suggests boldly I frame them
instead I burn you

                      in my cotton & linen
candle   is this a freedom feeling?
I moisturise my body twice & lie
back   arms wrapped around my knees
bent under my chin   I'm a roast chicken!
this is the closest I've been
to sex for some time & now your name is gone
I focus on the sounds I love: milk globbing
pasta squelching   like it's making out with itself

    & my favourite bits of quiet like
soft foods in the library: ham sandwich
ripe brown banana   thick berry smoothie
the wide-open space around sound
I think maybe now I could actually possibly
really maybe be
cycling home – brief montage – & to my back
            daytime fireworks
epiphany   epiphany

One Hard Star

sometimes I forget my eyes have a body
so busy I am in my seeing / my
being outside the party / fagless &
looking inside / my concave affection
like every time I try to be butch
as a pinstripe & fail / walking home with
the chicken / tender of neck / each bite to
the bone becomes the picture of each
bitten moon / reflected in the puddle
I step over / & the split in my lip grows
back over / or back together / gauzier
now than ever / this broken desire
machine / I'll be mean forever

PINK

I have done nothing today but peel grapes
& bleed   even the silver balloon
quivering in the wind looks down on me
when its course is blocked by the outstretched
arms of some wide tree I think   it's all good
everyone gets what they deserve in the end
I bet you would   help me on my way to
standing under the cherry blossom when
the wind blows   feeling my femme fantasy
I feel like a deer in the headlights of love
followed by *dynamic stance* followed by
half-heartedly coming out to my mum
like   *rape didn't make me gay*   but it sure
helped me on my way to   all these pink feels

Chill

       left the fallow fields of acid yellow
       rape behind & find myself   quite certain
       between two humming cars   their bodies
       winking in the sun's light   I find a patch
           raise my neck to it   & feel angelic
       for the first time since my moon blood
       soiled every white sheet left on the line
       my SE LDN soundtrack sounds like every
       pedal bike   softly grazing everybody
           of a car   did I already say how
       fleeting they are?   & in my spot of sun
       I recall all this death I've overcome
       just to be alive   somewhere   between
       two cars   –   but not overrun

modern derailleur types

the first conker shelled from
its bomber suit
flung across a rusty floor spiking
the bike tyre flat
flat on my back i heard the ribs
crack i say to dr paul who says
it will hurt a lot until it doesn't
& when you think you're fine
you'll crack again
boredom stretches out in front of me
like a rolled-out red carpet & time
rides in on a tortoise
making base camp with the weed
& the codeine makes me silly
my asshole itchy i google it
unsuccessfully
i burnt my hat last night
& the broomstick
i tell visiting friends i've completed
the internet & in absence of
any sense of self
start dropping stinking facts like
a video of the dehydrated moth
stealing the tears of baby birds
as they sleep i close the window
when my eyes wrinkle
at night a leaflet arrives from the church saying
mankind is thirsty & i think they mean
the moths my partner is upset that
i can't fuck him back there is an imbalance
he says *mankind is thirsty*
i think my cunt woke me up last night
it speaks & has a consciousness now
i close all the windows in the house
& sit in front of one a two-way
installation of boredom of fear

of moths i want to give you the
window seat & all my badus i want to
see this one through
swapping places i hear a crack
& have to wait to be airlifted
back to bed i ask my mum to
shower me she feeds me
from her mouth i go to sleep
thinking of the hairy moth
close to my face & crack
again as i lie still i
think my cunt gave a lecture on trauma
attendance was poor
next time i wake up halfway through
climbing out of an egg there are
skeletal wings starting to sprout
where my arms used to be
& the eggshell cracks
i leave the carcass behind but
today i have run out of
facts & people point at the wings
which i cannot yet address
but what of flight & i am
throwing the windows open dramatically
coaxing the moths in with lamps
looking my partner in the eye
as we fuck together gently
i think my cunt pulled its socks up
my lungs bellow freely throwing no caution to
clipping the sprouting wings back being
back on my bike seeing the hill through
the conkers gone & waiting expectantly
for surely i am never dust
& will outlive this one, too

DESHAWN MCKINNEY

Deshawn McKinney is an artist from Milwaukee, Wisconsin. His work is grounded in hip-hop and is a means of exploring liberation as multitudinous existence. Primarily engaged in grassroots organising for the past five years, he has been happy to re-centre his artistic praxis completing the MA Poetry at the UEA.

dmckinney.writer@gmail.com

Alternative Facts Intro

how bullets ate him
alive; Kennedy was the
first Black president.

—

Black life matter. on beat and off
beat no beat the heart still beat, police don't
badge be body camera enough. undercover
suv the hue of Huey – irony doesn't exist cuz he still
does. Hov doesn't exist but Shawn Carter does
                                              like
                                                      the louvre
    or
                    the tate modern

pieces of renaissance in the ghetto, birds overhead just
feathers. teachers propel us to excel cuz there's no cell
to push us into lynch you has no meaning, gardens untainted
with strange fruit. hoods on Black heads are just hoods
and neighborhoods never become them

We are,
a united State.

—

       scene: a flag
flutters in blunt smoke;
it will finish burning before the articles
of confederation supernova
                                                            our first
reality star.

hamilton prepares to die like Grant (Oscar); every death is a duel
with something. Billy Lee will die a free shadow, like shakespeare
if he looked like

Django   like hair like slave   like North Star

like wade in water   just cuz

                                                                                                      freedom

                    cuz his homie
                          would

– washington will be   our last king –

a predator drone hovers somewhere above

the 2nd amendment. the Fruit of Islam descends
in a siege of starched blue, as the patriots must have
at yorktown, they trample the boxwoods and robert e lee
becomes radicalized before he is conceived   freedom

comes at a price they say. martha is found in a spider hole

unfit for a first lady; it is near enough mount vernon   where you left her

over-seeing all that darkness, to be a guest room. she smells of hemp,
a last ditch effort to salve old tobacco wounds

but today, slaves choose   sober work the fields in   Off-White

robes, a solar eclipse. a flag flutters, a   blue black Shadow

asks if father taught her how to stare

directly into a   black hole

before being buried in one

On Appropriation

windswept and champagne-footed your sanctimony
rings hollow here. to thrift shop the culture
and expect the judge to hear your testimony

bold. you speak with carrion in your grill, vulture
the blood diamonds you call drip
do not make you worth our sculptures

we see you, flaunting your paid 'n full lips
safe in your alabaster fur, it looks   cheap
at least enough to hear the hook when it rips

off, we hear hints of miley in what you reap
(the notes bubble to a whisper then take flight)
as we watch your bones crumble themselves to sleep

go gently, though we know you want to mount a fight,
go gently, into that Black, all the parts you don't like.

Hair as Day Hike

Forest
my cliché is my hair
a freedom forest, dense
as the Mississippi wind
that sweltered my grandmother
to a God fearing; my curls
have grown collection plate full
creeping skyward like slabs
for Babel, holy holy

Camp
when I am next on my knees
do let your fingers take
the long trail – leave nothing
of bread crumbs, the best paths are
                                    un-
chartered

Clearing
my cliché is my hair
a clearing wrapped in black
satin, tinted window
of a North(side) Star; I untie
a flood this morning, Ark
at the barbershop, leave w/line up
like Woodstock*

                                * *here, Woodstock is a Black sea parted
from its Uncle Sam. some speakers are
submerged but everything is
insured (of course Kaepernick's settle-
ment money of course) we drip – they drown
and wave   appropriately.*

and hell followed with it

my friends are ghosts
of women who used to be
before men made them
into heroes – made them blood
of Christ sacrifice upon oath altars
bred from phallacy, under the heat
                            laughter

indelible to memory

martyrs before they can speak. before memory
warms to them enough to memorize their name
we hold trial to change it – they be
survivor: braveherothankyou
by the time they dig deep enough to discover they were
someone, who had a name like love
from a mother's breath.

I hope for the day I look
and upon my eyes be a pale
horse, and on it a woman
whose name is Death come to
reclaim her time and the hell
that suckled her before Heaven,
before prayers dripped from her eyes
onto pillows and reports, before
survivor: braveherothankyou

my friends don't die, rather life
is too fickle a form for the fury
they want to be, now, but men
need heroes. they become public sacrifice
in the wake of those vying to become history;

they will one day be
second coming.

Build the Wall and White Men Will Pay For It

it need not be particularly tall, just too big
to fail. in areas where it is infeasible to build, we will position a man
asking for donations to his progressive tax fund
and there will be a peculiar lack
of write off receipts. he will wear a bespoke suit, tailored
to slim fitting perfection, tan enough to blend into the dust
kicked up by the approaching caravan. as of election night,
our volunteers put them between Broadway and South Street, boys
being Dylan Roofs and Brock Turners, moving fast.

                                                                     they seek asylum

from liberal snowflakes, but Kamala Harris
will display a cooked egg   sunny side up
on the senate floor to end the debate
on global warming:

                                                                        Spoiler

it's re–

asthechildrenprayforthechildrenprayforthechildrenprayforthechildren
prayforthechildrenprayforthechildrenprayforthechildrenprayforthechil
drenprayforthechildrenprayforthechildrenprayforthechildrenprayforth
prayforthechildrenprayforthechildrenprayforthechildrenprayforthechil
drenprayforthechildrenprayforthechildrenprayforthechildrenprayforth
echildrenprayforthechildrenprayforthechildrenprayforthechildrenpray
asthechildrenprayforthechildrenprayforthechildrenprayforthechildren
prayforthechildrenprayforthechildrenprayforthechildrenprayforthechil
drenprayforthechildrenprayforthechildrenprayforthechildrenprayforth
echildrenprayforthechildrenprayforthechildrenprayforthechildrenpray
asthechildrenprayforthechildrenprayforthechildrenprayforthechildren
prayforthechildrenprayforthechildrenprayforthechildrenprayforthechil
drenprayforthechildrenprayforthechildrenprayforthechildrenprayforth
echildrenprayforthechildrenprayforthechildrenprayforthechildrenpray
forthechildrenpray   for   the   children   pray fo

LAIA SALES MERINO

Laia Sales Merino is a poet from the Catalan Pyrenees. She is currently based in the UK. In her poetry, the English language coexists with Catalan, Spanish and any other language that has been on her mind (recently, Portuguese). Her work can be found in *Eyot*, *amberflora* and *Ambit*.

laiasm@outlook.com

rotura y p'arriba

my life was going one way & now is going another | whatever i do i end sobeando like Sofía in the midday culebrón | look me in the ojos & see promise after promise dripping on the table | i wanna hug him, kiss him, mi amor | can't call him mi amor anymore | mi corazón lo lloro | i am writing about the four años that we grew together | la Gina y la mama hugging me like i am this heart-pitted cosita & *ay lai, plora, plora* | i let my body caerse en el sofá | i turn la tele on | blanket tight keeping mi cuerpecito junto | i am sobeando cause la tele parla about trainspotting about scotland about you | tus scottish blue eyes vermellíssims bouncing everywhere in the living room & i cannot take this | been drinking triple tilas all day like la mama said | been llorando till there's no llàgrimes left | ah chica qué pasó | i squeezed love till it became amor | oye i surrender & life just move me wherever | 'entre dos aguas' is playing from my sister's room | my hips waving un poco & my fingers snapping un poquito | p'aquí y p'allá | mírame in the eyes | mi vida was going one way & now it can go many ways.

VOLAR

              pa mis hermanas, Gina y Sara, boniques

listening
to understand
  three bruised souls
ay, ya no we can't más
mirant-nos pel carrer sí per la street with
our eyes stuck on each other
fucking up our lungs even more y we
are in the city of la fantasy
la nostra of our art, sí, la cosa
of our hearts & when we fall
              if we fall
we are falling from this balcony into
the gold hours of Lisboa into
the sore sweet vida díselo SÍ el volar
              the flying of de Lucía vente p'acá
              watch us volar with every step
              watch us whisper *vámonos*

ao céu de lisboa
al cel de lisboa
al cielo de lis—

                              [Sara]
                Emmm dreams for my life right now?
                Pues the truth is that [chuckles]
            I try not to think about it much because...
           because no sé, is a complicated question.

no sabemos & we
don't know pero
we laugh we smoke we lift
each other from la calle
like princesas, mira
serpent ones, bonitas
como la mamá
    because no sé
    but tonight we're out & up

       for un amanecer in your flat, nossos amores if
       we find you & who knows
       i mean look at us
       el cielo broken broken our eyes
       los pinares in our hearts siempre
       tres souls amoratadísimas
           the dawn from yours, our tonight loves
           or wherever we want to be
           SÍ we climb up the hills of this cidade
           in sneakers & Humana skirts
           ay ay ay una birra & some lunalike thing
                una birra & another y otra
                un cigarro y otro y otro y otro
                (*mejor que sobre que no que falte, no?*)
que sobre, que sobre cause these people
   with their guitarras & their hearts cantando out their mouths
      cause these people too live to the rhythm of palmas & olés

                                    [Gina]
               Bueno whenever they ask me this,
                        it's being happy.
              It seems cursi but it's true, eh?
     En plan I don't care with whom, how or where
                      but being happy...

qué escandalooosas!   we are
here   being happy ay sí
sipping three hot chocolates
reading for each other
the kids' books in Menina e Moça
in our Portuguese we let it drip
slow into our tongues & next year
falamos ya perfectamente eh
clar que sí
talkeando about our loves
      [Gina] & *this girl que me tiene enamorá!*
      [Sara] & *this boy que no vamo a separá!*
      [Laia] & *my heart pobre ya no puede má!*
& you are there   on my mind with
your candle-lighting shit, tus hoodies
your preguntas, pero y qué

  leaning in, into
   the love, falling from the balcony
    & who cares
       but i care
    but i guess
    que lo entiendo baby lo entiendo.
                [Sara]
      I guess I hope to be able to live in many different places
      en plan get to know many different lifestyles & cultures
       & also I would like pues to help people in some way.
Sarins   Sareta
keepinglo red so rojo los chavales
get burnt no?
if se acercan bad & don't
respect, joder   & you
your wildfuego tre tus ribs y tú
in Argentina now, then donde sea
que brille sacred, bright forever
your fuego, your arte, then wherever
it feels good & it feels
      good now right?
      bodies meneando
      alegría   we are
      coming like reinas
      rotas, maybe, pero mira
      el gold en la rotura, SÍ
      el oro!
& we fall asleep
in the middle of Lisboa under a greyoso sky & on top of our scarves
Sara's hair around her like a halo
Gina's eyelids like el sol brillant
de la vall y mis orejas hurting silver we are
talking, talking, twitching
   serpientes por tós laos *serpientes & the sun nowhere*
this park now with women everywhere our ghostly loves
l'àvia i la besàvia i la Marina i la Clàudia i la Daria i la Mercedes i la Paula i la Laura i

94

>   *mujeres, mujeres...*
>   *mama, mama...*
>   *ay lo que haremos...*

& we wake up our ojos charged with la nostra història.

>   [Gina]
>   *Que mais, que mais?*
>   *Through art being able to help people*
>   *& to earn enough money doing what I love.*
>   *Ehhh I think that ja està,*
>   *these are my dreams.*

Yin, with your somnis with
these alas de oro
stirring you on
with your talisman ojos blessing us since
always with your analògiques loving
all of us volando in gold, volando aware
absorbing every day more directly, you are free
to love whoever & tell whoever to fuck off
with ese canturreo d'artistassa dale
Yin, with your heart-wings, wearing your 300 rings
que mais, que mais?
>   but baby i'm drunk (*así no, así no*)
>   & everything is about you now   fuck
>   *fóllame y luego miénteme, miénteme*
>   lento, lento, con tus ojos negros
>   pero tú no mientes, no mientes
>   but no we don't hurt no? we don't
>   ayyy
>   with our eyes stuck
>   pero vamos a amar that yes
>   that first   & well

but Yin, with your heart-rings, wearing your 300 wings,
que mais?

                                                      & i guess

that i just want una jodida table to write
& some space to move
& some sun
y amor everywhere
that i wanna live everywhere
that i wanna vivir a mi aire volar que yo quiero volar quiero vivir volando
y volar a mi aire

        but talking with you, boniques
        you want to
        live como okupas
        i don't know
        if i can do it
        but i love you
        i'll be there
        somehow   listening

to understand / we are falling from this balcony / is a complicated question / y no sabemos no sabemos no / but we cook rice soup for each other / *dios què bo!* / we carry each other whenever & wherever / we shave each other's hair / these músics de carrer pacing our movement round the city / & wind's moving all the dresses, art & earrings in the market / ay these three bruised souls & some lunalike thing / pero ahora being happy ay sí / míranos / loving so well so well (*así no, así no*) / & you are there like a like a – fuck, pero y qué
        & que mais
        y what més
        & que else volando aware i guess with care pero
        volando, SÍ
                ao céu de lisboa
                al cel de lisboa
                al cielo de lisboa
                                y que mais, eh?
                                que mais?

RYAN NORMAN

Ryan Norman has been a poet-in-residence in St George's Gardens, London, and his work has appeared in *The Cadaverine*, the Poetry School Mixed Borders Pamphlet, *Black Bough Poetry* and *The Mancunion*.

ryannorman1995@hotmail.co.uk.

Construction

I walk through a city built by newspapers

they write how I know the world

like world-builders
towers print themselves
over sun
like redacted documents

roads spin out
a line through haze
like light
calling loosely over waves
to somewhere I can be sure
of what I'm told
about rock

so wind writes itself
into these unintended crevices of highstreets
echoes cold between scaffolded tubes
        nudges me towards
soft options
warm behind panes of glass

concrete clenches itself
against outstretched palms
shoves cold up into knees
        bent over pavements
only rags to keep them from acting out
            its bitter light

signs direct to designated areas
        where people fold   into smoke

        trace themselves through sirens

twist into a reason to dissipate

or stain themselves against a chosen wall

streets weep for direction
written into the air by passers-by
      to kiss a spine into routes
flexing through their arrangement of concrete's fact

looked-for knowledge

decided on by the reach

        of threaded white lines

        or a draught whispering
        through blinds

since through it all
people live out the ideas
printed at the end of whistled noises

lines followed through mist
to parks studded with lights over gaping benches
      they might arrive
shirts stained by the wind
fresh to the smell of wet grass
wondering which bench to bring to life
which swelling of dew-peppered fruit to pick from shrubs
what happens in the margins scattered between the lights
what the empty swings might know about you
or what the scratchy path suggests about your soles
how you know your weight
how their world knows it

        and what the two of you might make of it together
        creaking through oaken dark
        or dawn

RAF Boxing Association

Grandad smacked the weight of a sawdust bag,
shirtless, young in the gape

              of a disused hangar,

smashed gloves into dullness to prise open
the burden of things thrown where mothers

              hide their eyes.

He punched alone by abandoned propellers;
new planes deserving a wild bloom left

              blasted in by artillery,

dented youths silent in windy fumes, squat beside
freshly spun up brothers rolling out to track

              strange directions of light

on engines quivering like infants, felt preciously
by engineers who wrapped their hulks like blankets

              to keep out the world.

On flight; clanged to scraps, shredded
over mats of cloud like ribbons

              of babywear

flung back in a mother's face. At base; Grandad
worked the bag, cut up into its core, asked

              more of himself

than flakes of sawdust beat from the nuzzle
of a stitch's breast. Its fabric, torn,

        whimpered for lost flakes,

ached to nestle them in her wrapped self,
soak up shots, let them swing from her chain

        unharmed

while she knew everything about punches.
Fluttered by beaten out sawdust,

        Grandad sweated away,

freshly introduced to a world. Somewhere,
his first opponent does the same, young. Somewhere,

        his mother

knows.

Community

At Christmas, our church performed sketches
and interpretive dance at their cabaret.
Every year, stage-light
swelled the hall's margins,
warmed us along the pews,
but the night two girls sang Elton John
the room's corners darkened
into themselves, left
us sat cold by stony
walls. Halfway
through their song
a woman fell down in a fit,
threw her limbs
at herself, hit
the floor hard.
But nobody stared
as her family gathered round,
made her warm with coats as the girls sang on,
their notes making room for her crashes
like a refusal; spread by fresh light
around the hall.

Undone

Under us, Yosemite's glaciers
have questioned everything.

We've had them forget what they love,
let the granite peel away its belief in ice

like undressing, reluctantly. *We took
its walls down in the sun* and exposed

the valley to its light, left it ashamed
of the wind on its face, in its streams,

through the bare pines.
Muir said he'd know the glaciers,

how they thickened over Lyell's peak,
worked in silence on the mountains

he climbed. I'd have followed him,
measured the ice's trust in the mountains

with pinewood stakes, before the land
suspected its own bedrock,

back when the park held itself close
and glaciers left fields, waiting for forests.[1]

---

[1] This poem is informed by, and quotes from, an article in the *New York Tribune* from December 5th, 1871, by John Muir

crawl

what do we build
to the hollow ring of iron plates
knocked against themselves
damp fabric spread over our backs
panting to rubber floors
that offer no comfort
to abandoned dumbbells
or spilled water
kilos arranged along the bar
as we lay down to press
over and over
until we're lifted out of ourselves
and into Daniel Craig
climbing from the waves
rippled lines set
in blue trunks to perform
his new shape of man
one we crawl towards
to bear the weight
we don't choose to lift

Acknowledgements

Thanks are in order for the School of Literature, Drama and Creative Writing at UEA in partnership with Egg Box Publishing for making the MA Creative Writing anthologies possible.

Tiffany Atkinson, Vahni Capildeo, Sarah Gooderson, Rachel Hore, Michael Lengsfield, Kate Mattocks, Sandy Pool, Meryl Pugh, Sophie Robinson, Cecilia Rossi, Jos Smith, Jeremy Noel-Tod.

Nathan Hamilton at UEA Publishing Project, and Emily Benton.

Editorial Committee:
    Taylor Beidler
    Amber Higgins
    Judith Khan
    Jasmin Kirkbride
    Poppy Kleiser
    Deshawn McKinney
    Jon Platten

With grateful thanks to all the funders who make possible the scholarships that support our poets.

UEA MA Creative Writing Anthologies: Poetry, 2019

First published by Egg Box Publishing, 2019
Part of UEA Publishing Project Ltd.

International © 2019 retained by individual authors

This book is sold subject to the condition that it shall not, by way of trade or otherwise, be lent, resold, hired out, stored in a retrieval system, or otherwise circulated without the publisher's prior consent in any form of binding or cover other than that in which it is published and without a similar condition including this condition being imposed on the subsequent purchaser.

A CIP record for this book is available from the British Library
Printed and bound in the UK by Imprint Digital

Designed by Emily Benton Book Design
emilybentonbookdesigner.co.uk

Proofread by Sarah Gooderson

Distributed by NBN International
10 Thornbury Road Plymouth
PL6 7PP
+44 (0)1752 202301
e.cservs@nbninternational.com

ISBN: 978-1-911343-71-4